1·2·3 Draw

Pets and Farm Animals

A step by step guide

by
Freddie
Levin

Peel Productions, Inc.

Before you begin

You will need:

1. a pencil

2. an eraser

3. a pencil sharpener

4. lots of paper (recycle and re-use!)

5. colored pencils

6. a folder for saving work

7. a comfortable place to draw

8. good light

Now let's begin...!

Published by Peel Productions, Inc.
Printed in China.

Library of Congress Cataloging-in-Publication Data

Levin, Freddie.
    1-2-3 draw pets and farm animals / by Freddie Levin.
        p. cm.
    Includes index.
    ISBN 0-939217-40-6
        1. Domestic animals in art--Juvenile literature. 2. Drawing--Technique--Juvenile
    literature. [1. Domestic animals in art. 2. Animals in art. 3. Drawing--Technique.] I.
    Title: One-two-three draw pets and farm animals. II. Title.

NC783.8.D65 L48 2000

743.6--dc21   00-055072

Distributed to the trade and art markets in North America by

NORTH LIGHT BOOKS,
an imprint of F&W Publications, Inc.
4700 East Galbraith Road
Cincinnati, OH 45236

(800) 289-0963

Contents

Important drawing tip number 1:

*** Draw lightly at first, so you can erase extra lines ***

Important drawing tip number 2:

*** Have fun drawing pets and farm animals! ***

Important drawing tip number 3:

*** Practice makes better ***

Circles, Ovals and Eggs

The drawings in this book start with three basic shapes:

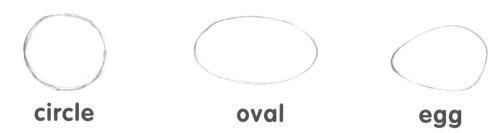

circle   **oval**   **egg**

*A circle is perfectly round.

*An oval is a squashed circle.

*An egg is an oval with one side fatter than the other.

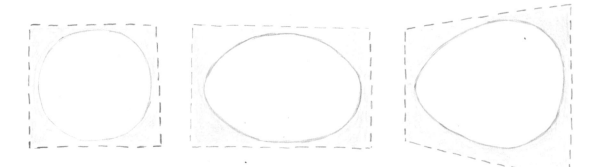

A **circle**
fits inside
a square.

An **oval**
fits inside
a rectangle.

An **egg**
fits inside
a trapezoid.

The more you practice drawing **circles, ovals** and **eggs,** the easier it will be.

Remember:

Draw lightly!

Note to parents and teachers:
I have found it helpful in working with very young children with poorly developed motor control to have them begin their drawings by tracing a small cardboard cutout of an egg, oval, or circle.

Cat

1 Draw a **circle** and an **egg**.

2 Connect them with two curved lines.

3 Add triangle ears and two legs.

4 Add two more legs and a tail.

DRAW LIGHTLY!

5 Add two eyes and a triangle nose.

6 Erase the extra lines.

7 Draw a mouth and whiskers. Add stripes. Color your cat.

A cat can be a great pet. Cats like to cuddle and play. When they are happy, you can hear them purr.

Sitting Cat

1 Draw a **circle** above an **egg**.

2 Add triangle ears. Draw two front legs.

3 Add eyes, a triangle nose and a mouth.

Add small back feet.

4 Draw whiskers. Add a tail. Shade ears. Erase extra lines!

About Cats

Spotted cats are called **Calico cats**.

Striped cats are called **Tabby cats**.

This cat is a **Scaredy cat!**

Draw a catnip mouse for **your** cat!

1

2

3

Dog

1 Draw a **circle** and an **egg**.

2 Add two triangle ears and the neck.

Dogs are wonderful friends. Dogs that live in your home can seem like part of the family.

3 Now draw two legs.

Some dogs do important jobs. Some help the disabled and others guide the sightless.

4 Draw a stubby tail. Add two eyes, and two more legs.

5 Add lines for the markings on the face and legs. Draw a nose and a mouth.

6 Erase extra lines and shade dark areas. Draw a collar for your dog.

This dog looks ready to play ball. Draw a ball and a rubber bone for your dog.

Sitting Dog

1 Draw a **circle** above an **egg**. Notice that they **overlap**.

2 Add two floppy ears. Draw two eyes.

3 Draw a triangle nose. Add two front paws.

4 Draw the mouth and back legs.

5 Shade ears. Draw lines for toes. Erase extra lines and color your dog.

Good dog!

Rabbit

Start with a **circle** on top of an **egg.**

2 Draw two long ears and two eyes.

3 Add a nose, front feet, back feet, and a tail.

4 Draw a mouth. Add lines for toes, and make the tail fluffy. Erase extra lines. Add color.

Idea!
Make a carrot for your rabbit.

Another Rabbit

1 Draw a **circle** on top of an **egg.**

2 Add one ear, one eye. and a fluffy tail.

3 Add another ear and a nose. Draw two feet.

4 Put lines in the ears and draw a mouth. Draw another front foot.

5 Erase extra lines and add color!

A rabbit can be a peaceful, gentle pet.

Parakeet

1 Start with a **circle** and an **egg.**

2 Draw a circle for the eye. Connect the head and body with curved lines.

Add the flight feathers.

3 Draw a beak. Shade the eye. Add a tail. Draw two feet.

4 Draw stripes on the head and wings. Add dots near the beak. Color the tummy, tail and beak.

Lively, colorful parakeets are the most popular pet bird. With patience and gentle handling, they can become very tame, learn tricks and even speak a few words.

5 Erase extra lines. Give your parakeet a perch.

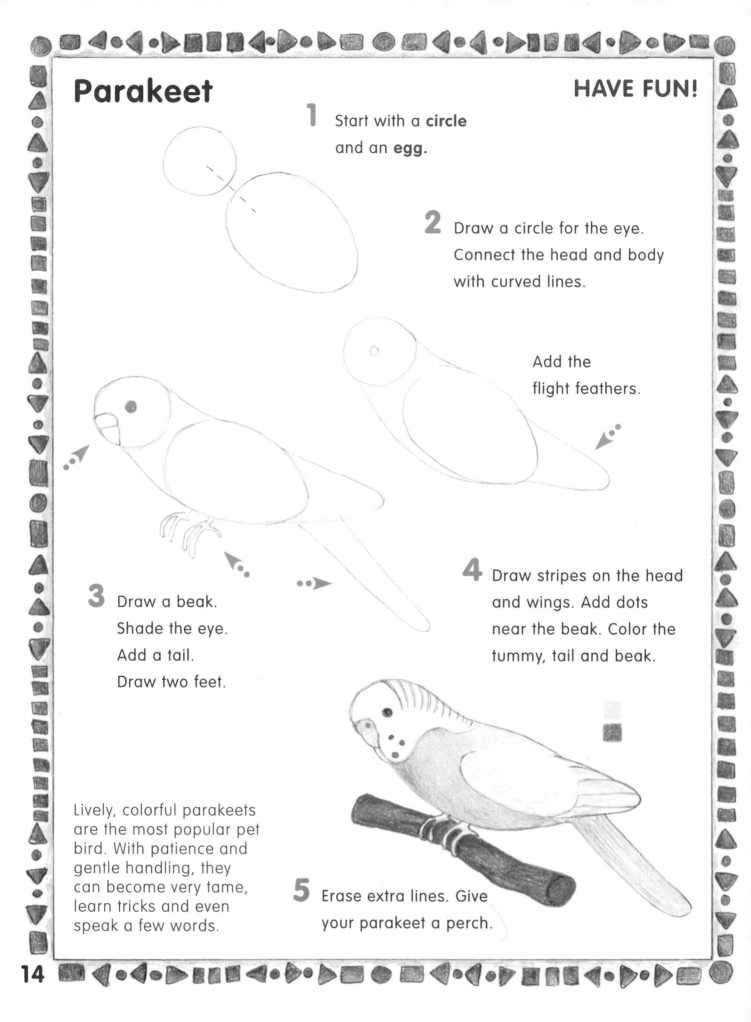

14

Canary

1 Draw a **circle** and **egg**. Make them **overlap**.

2 Add a wing shape.

3 Draw an eye and a pointy beak.

4 Now draw a tail and two feet.

5 Erase extra lines and give your bird a perch. Color your canary.

Canaries have been kept as pets for hundreds of years. Male canaries have a beautiful rolling song.

Parrot

1 Start with a **circle** and an **egg.**

2 Add an eye and two curved lines for a neck.

3 Add a curved upper beak. Add wing feathers.

4 Draw the lower beak. Add tail feathers.

Parrots come in every color of the rainbow. They range in size from tiny parrotlets to great big macaws.

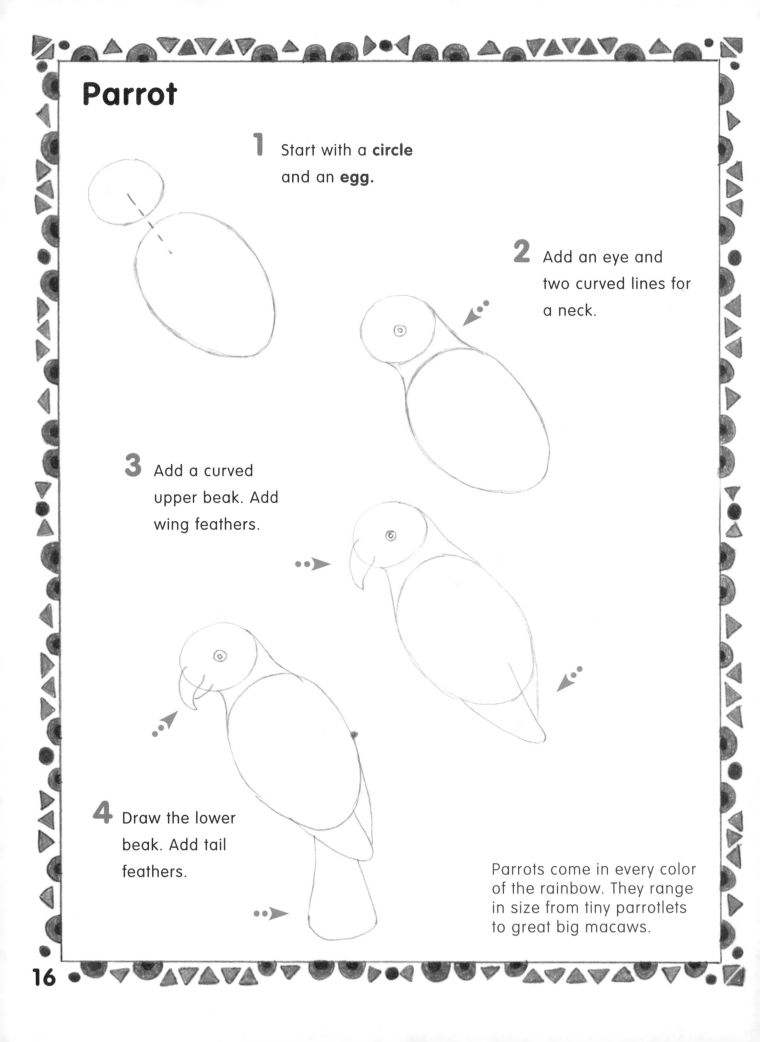

Parrots need special care to stay healthy and happy. They have long life spans. Some parrots can live fifty or sixty years.

5 Add the bump on a parrot's nose called a cere. Add feet.

6 Erase extra lines. Add shading and color the feathers. Add feather lines on wings and tail. Draw a perch for your parrot.

Many parrots are very intelligent. Parrots are well-known for their ability to mimic human speech.

Mouse

1 Draw a small **egg** and a large **egg**. Notice the angle of both.

2 Draw the neck with two curved lines. Add a circle for an eye.

3 Add a circle for the ear. Draw the nose.

4 Add the front leg.

Mice are thought of as household pests. However a mouse from a pet store can be a fun and lively animal to watch. They come in a variety of colors and are relatively easy to care for.

5 Add a long thin tail. Add a hind leg.

6 Draw the other ear. Make another front leg and hind leg.

1

2

3

Make some cheese for your mouse!

7 Add some whiskers. Erase extra lines. Add shading. Darken the eye.

Gerbil

A gerbil is a rodent, a cousin to the mouse. Gerbils have fur on their tails. Their strong hind legs make them good leapers.

1 Start with an **egg** and a **circle**. Notice the angles.

2 Connect the egg and circle with curved lines. Make a dot for the eye.

3 Add two ears and a nose.

4 Draw a tail. Add a nose line. Draw three legs.

5 Erase extra lines. Use short pencil strokes to make your gerbil look furry.

Guinea Pig

1 Draw two **eggs**, one larger than the other. Notice how they **overlap**.

Guinea pigs are not pigs and they are not from Guinea. They are rodents, like mice and hamsters.

2 Make a dot for the eye. Add two curved lines to form the neck

3 Add two ears. Draw feet.

4 Add whiskers. Draw lines for markings.

5 Erase extra lines and add color to your creation!

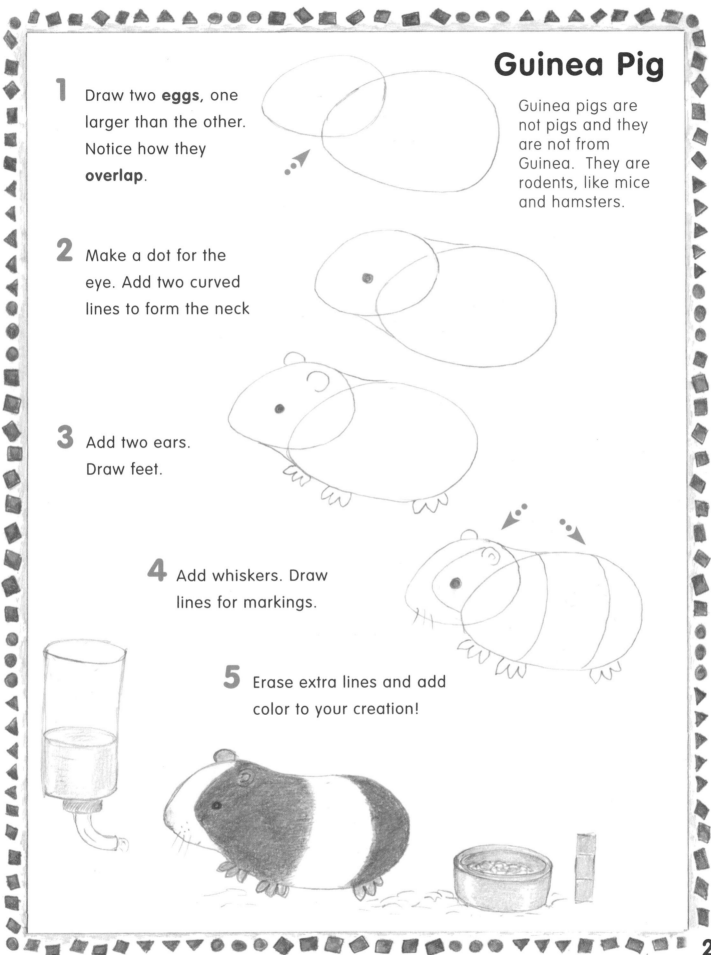

21

Hamster

1 Start with an **egg** and a **circle**. Notice the angle of the egg.

Hamsters are nocturnal creatures. They are active at night.

2 Draw a curved line connecting the egg and circle. Add a circle for the eye.

3 Draw two ears. Add the curve for the nose. Draw two hind feet.

4 Add another eye, nose and a front paw.

5 Make a second front paw. Add a stubby tail. Draw a line inside the ear.

6 Erase extra lines and add color and shading in the fur.

Happy hamster!

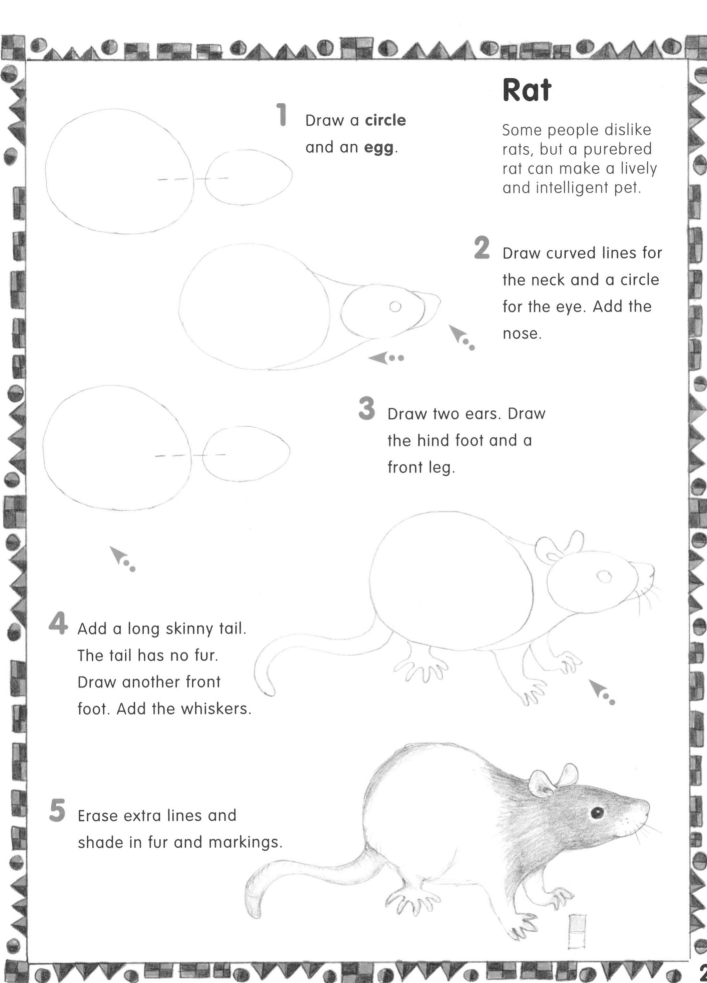

Rat

Some people dislike rats, but a purebred rat can make a lively and intelligent pet.

1 Draw a **circle** and an **egg**.

2 Draw curved lines for the neck and a circle for the eye. Add the nose.

3 Draw two ears. Draw the hind foot and a front leg.

4 Add a long skinny tail. The tail has no fur. Draw another front foot. Add the whiskers.

5 Erase extra lines and shade in fur and markings.

Iguana

1 Start with an **oval** and an **egg**.

2 Connect with curved lines, and draw the nose.

3 Add an eye bump, an eye, a nostril and a mouth.

4 Draw two legs.

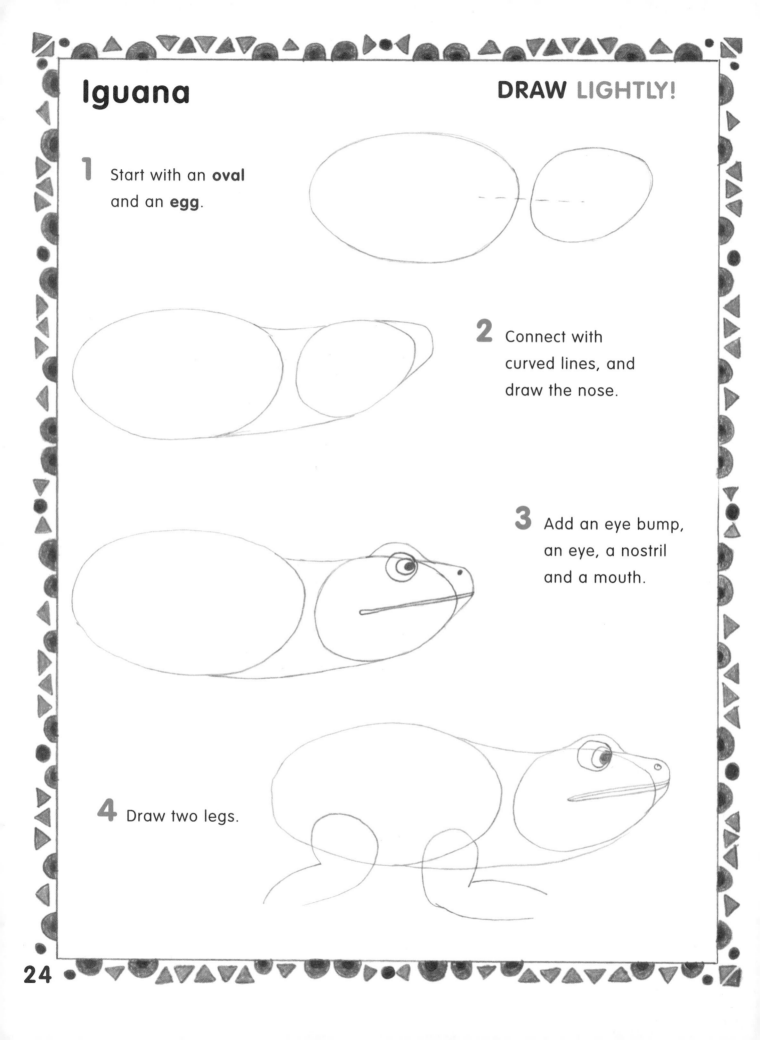

5 Add feet and claws.

6 Add a long curved tail. Draw bumpy scales on the back. Draw a wattle on the throat.

7 Erase extra lines. Color your iguana.

Iguanas can grow quite large.

It is best to get them when they are small and handle them daily to keep them tame.

Gecko

1 Start with two small **ovals**. Notice how far apart they are.

2 Connect ovals with curved lines. Add an eye.

3 Add a curved tail. Draw a curve for the nose.

4 Add a line for the mouth, and a dot for the nose. Draw legs and feet.

5 Erase extra lines and color the markings. Give your gecko some rocks and plants. *Great gecko!*

Geckos' suction cup-like feet let them scurry up walls.

Chameleon

Chameleons can change color. This helps them blend in with their surroundings.

1 Start with an **oval** and a **circle**.

2 Add the crest shape. Draw the eye and mouth. Add a line for the throat.

3 Draw a spiral tail.

4 Draw scales on the back, and add the legs.

5 Erase lines and color your chameleon.

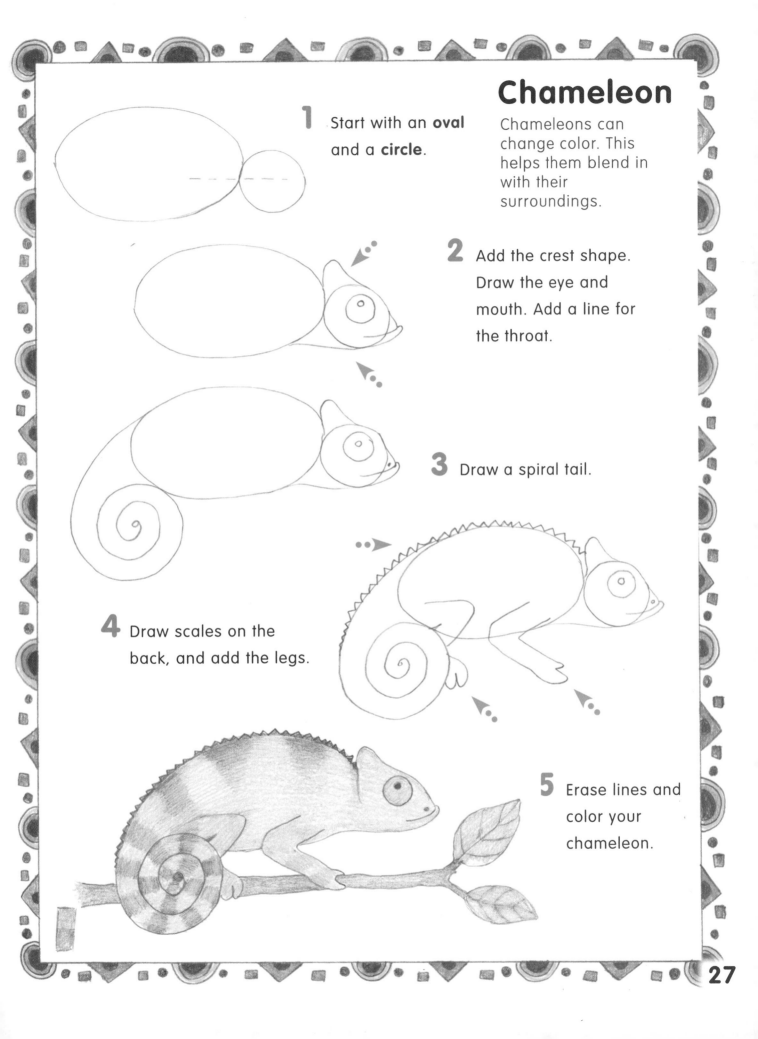

Turtle

1 Draw an **egg**.

2 Add lines on either end to make the shell shape.

3 Draw the head and neck.

4 Add an eye. Draw two legs.

5 Draw neck line, shell markings, and a tail. Add the lower shell called the plastron. Draw the toes.

6 Erase lines and add color.

Turtles have hard shells to protect them. Turtles have been on Earth since the time of the dinosaurs.

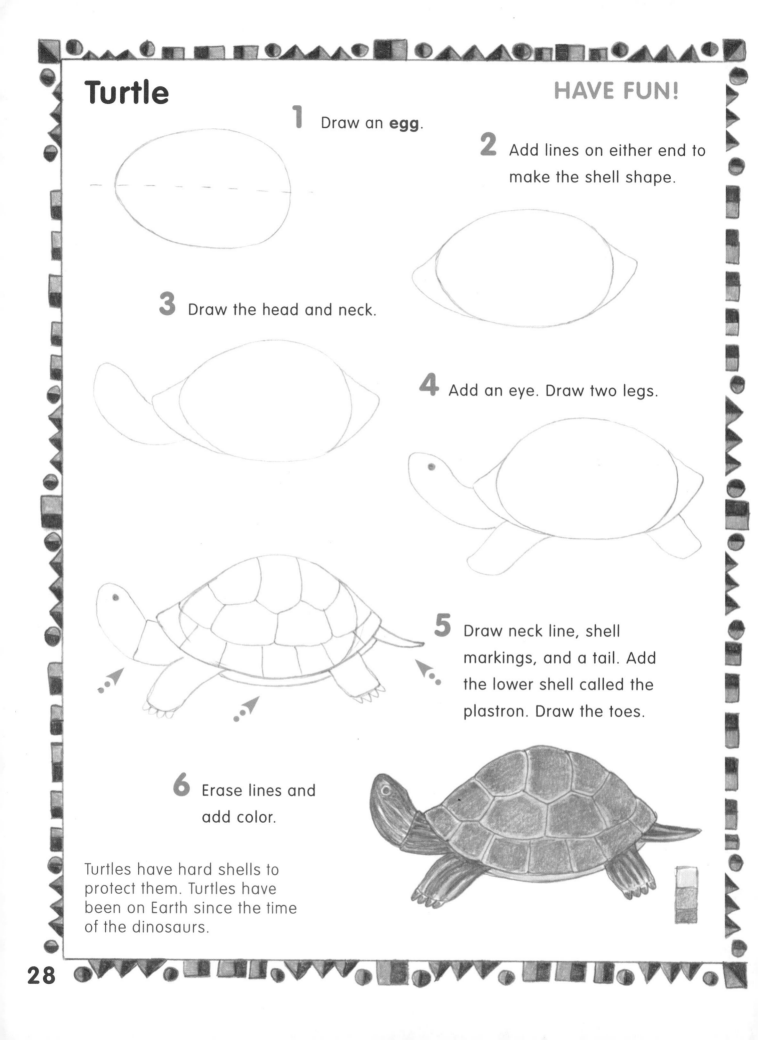

28

Frog

1 Draw two **eggs**, one larger than the other.

2 Draw a **circle** for the eye. Add another egg inside the large egg.

Frogs are amphibians. That means they can breathe in water and air.

3 Draw two neck lines, and a leg line.

4 Add a mouth. Draw feet and legs.

5 Add a bump for the other eye. Draw the eye and nose.

6 Erase lines and add color.

Frogs start out as tadpoles.

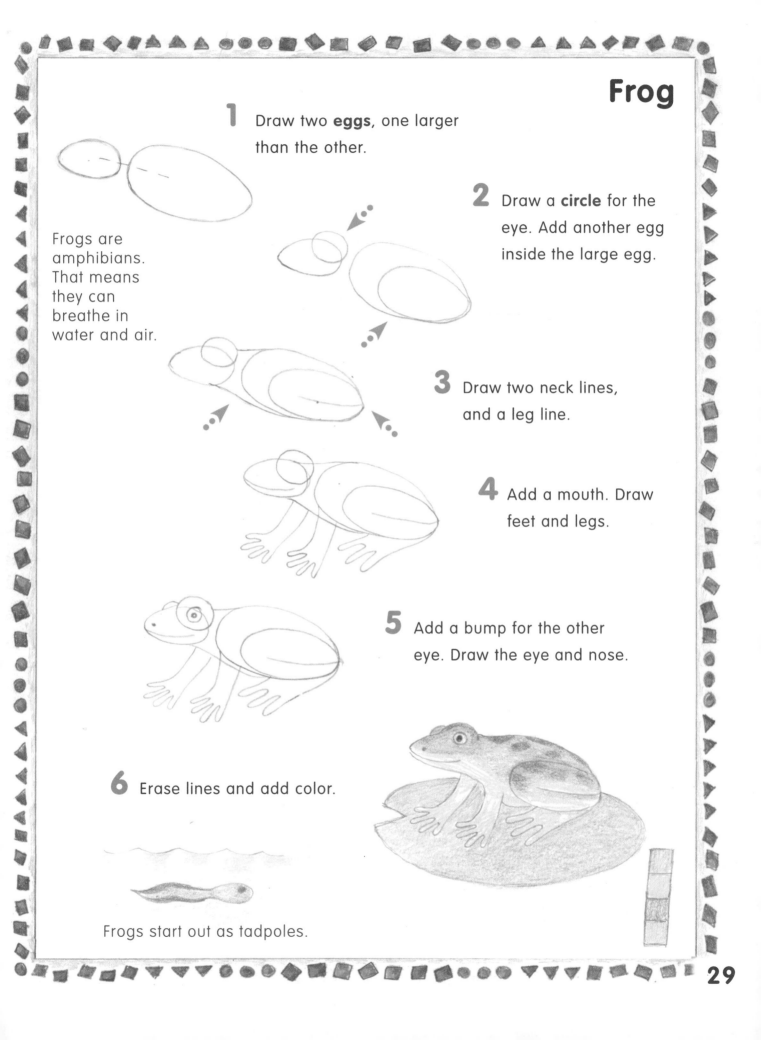

Goldfish

1 Start with an **oval**.

2 Add an eye and a curve for the face.

3 Draw a **circle** around the eye. Add a dorsal fin.

4 Draw a gill and add three more fins.

5 Draw a fancy tail.

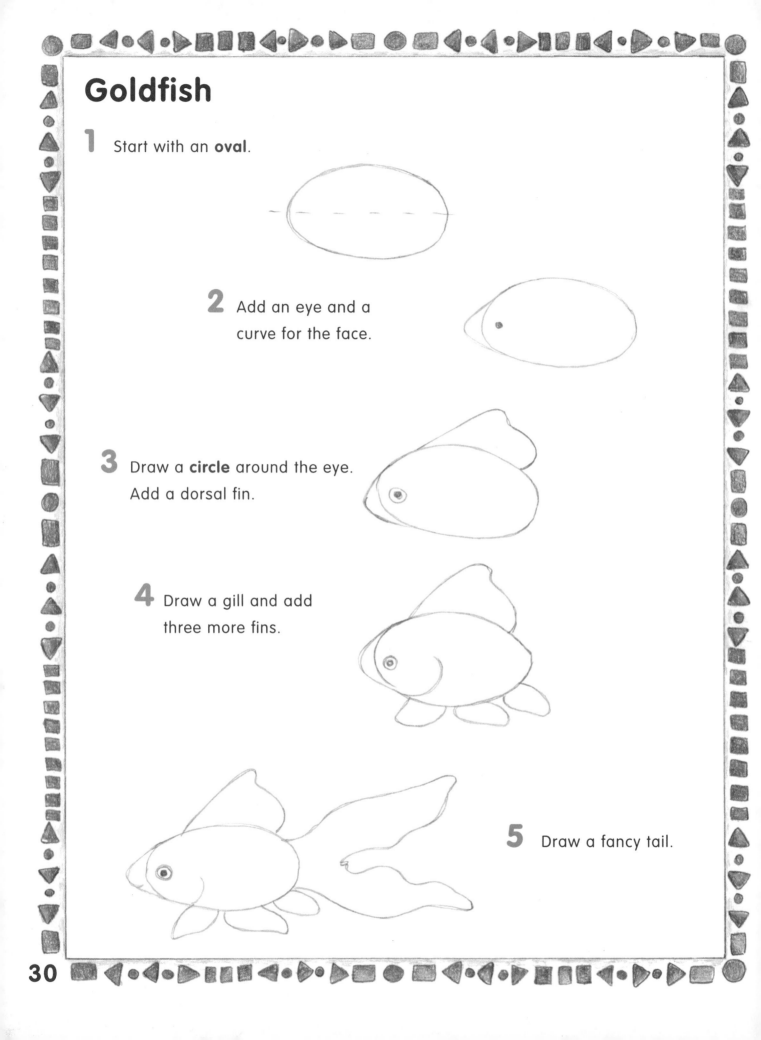

6 Erase extra lines. Shade in scales and markings. Make a bowl for your goldfish. Add some pebbles and a plant.

Goldfish need to swim in cold water. A heated tank would make them sick. Some goldfish live outside in ponds.

Aquarium Fish
Angel Fish

1 Draw a **circle**.

2 Draw the face. Add an eye.

3 Add fins and mouth.

4 Add barbels.

5 Draw a tail fin.

6 Add fin lines and shading.

Tiger Barb

1 Start with an **oval**.

2 Add tail and head.

3 Draw two fins.

4 Finish markings.

Zebra Danio

1 Draw an **oval**.

2 Add tail. Draw the head and eye.

3 Add stripes and gill line.

Make an aquarium for your fish. Add rocks and plants.

Ferret

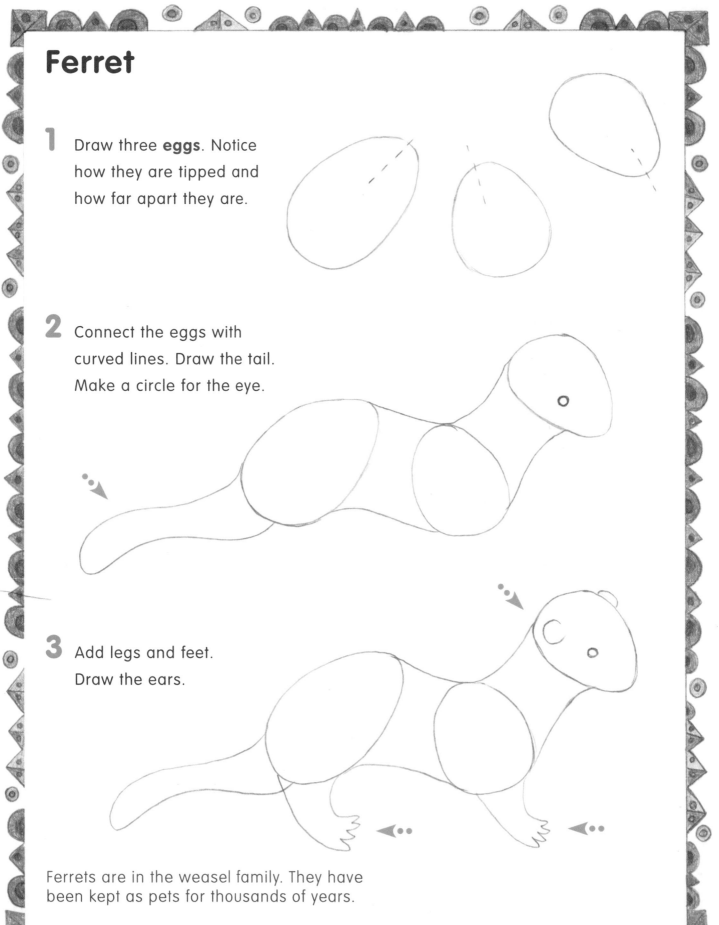

1 Draw three **eggs**. Notice how they are tipped and how far apart they are.

2 Connect the eggs with curved lines. Draw the tail. Make a circle for the eye.

3 Add legs and feet. Draw the ears.

Ferrets are in the weasel family. They have been kept as pets for thousands of years.

4 Add another eye and darken both eyes. Draw the nose and mouth. Add another foot.

5 Erase extra lines. Shade in markings. With short pencil strokes, draw fur. Draw the ferret's "bandit mask."

Fun ferret!

Make some toys for your playful ferret.

Tarantula

Not everybody might think a big, hairy spider would make a great pet.

However, they have become such popular terrarium animals that certain species have had to be protected in the wild lest they disappear.

1 Start with an **egg** and an **oval**.

2 Draw the start of four legs.

3 Start four more legs and draw six eyes.

4 Complete four legs. Add a mouth.

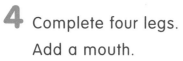

5 Finish two more legs.

6 Add two palps, which catch and hold prey.

Erase extra lines. Add shading. Use short pencil strokes to make your spider hairy!

Pigeon

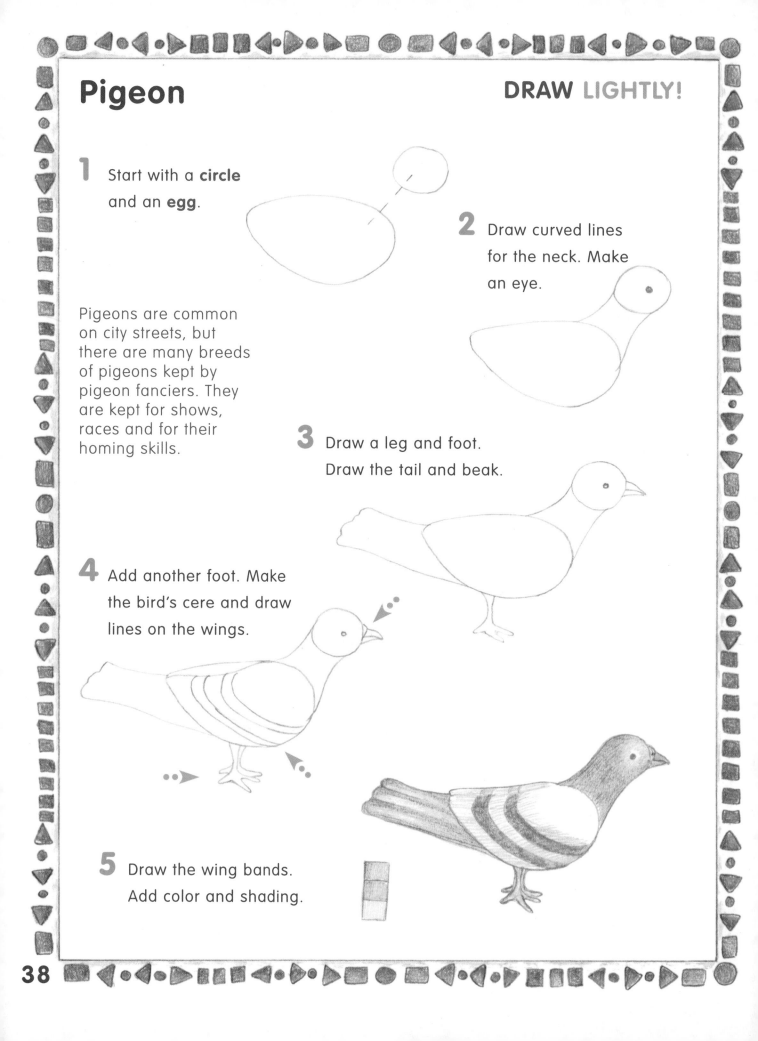

DRAW LIGHTLY!

1 Start with a **circle** and an **egg**.

Pigeons are common on city streets, but there are many breeds of pigeons kept by pigeon fanciers. They are kept for shows, races and for their homing skills.

2 Draw curved lines for the neck. Make an eye.

3 Draw a leg and foot. Draw the tail and beak.

4 Add another foot. Make the bird's cere and draw lines on the wings.

5 Draw the wing bands. Add color and shading.

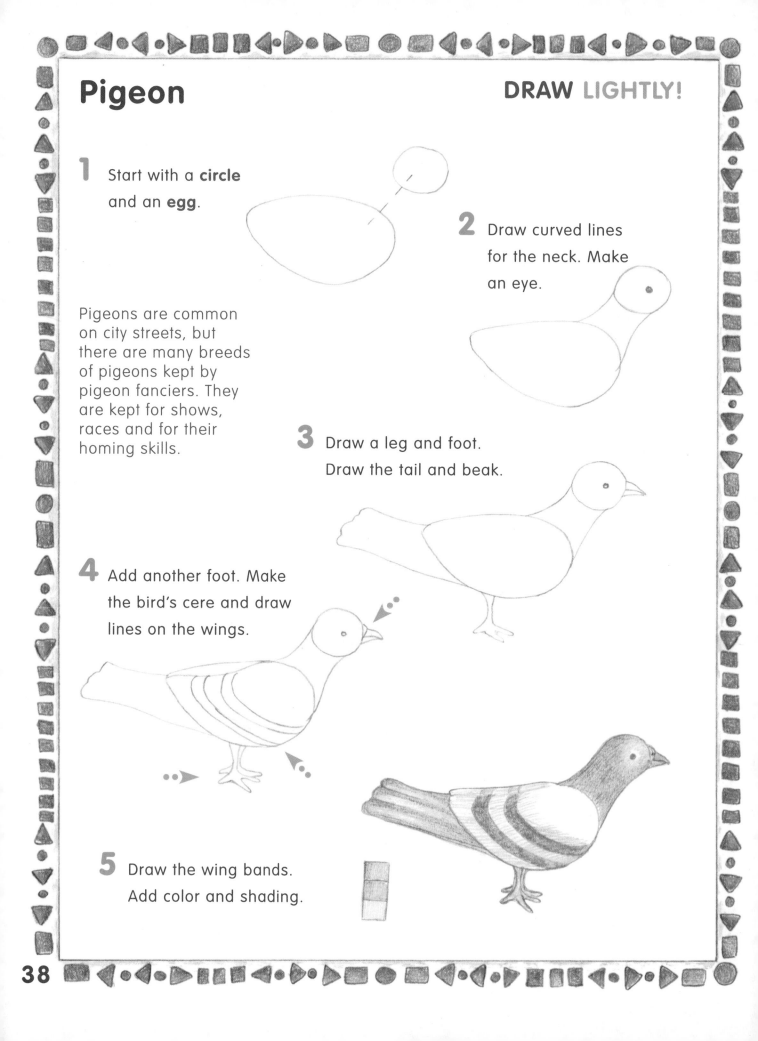

Pig

1 Start with a **circle** and an **oval**. Notice how they **overlap**.

2 Draw two legs. Add two eyes and the snout.

3 Draw the other two legs. Add two ears. Add two nostrils.

4 Erase extra lines. Add a curly tail and shading. Color spots and hooves.

Pretty pig!

Pigs are smart animals. They can learn tricks like dogs. Pigs are not dirty animals, but roll in mud to protect their skin from sunburn.

Sheep

1 Start with an **oval** and a **circle**.

2 Add ears and an eye.

3 Draw the nose. Draw two legs.

Sheep have warm, woolly coats. The wool is sheared in the spring. This does not hurt the sheep—it is like a haircut. The wool is spun into yarn and then made into warm hats, sweaters, mittens, and blankets.

4 Draw a little tail. Draw a line to form the face. Add two more legs.

5 Draw the inner ears. Add the neck. Draw hooves. Make your sheep woolly. Erase extra lines and add shading.

People have been herding sheep from before Biblical times.

Goat

1 Start with a big **egg** and a small **egg**.

2 Connect head and body with neck lines. Add two eyes.

3 Draw two legs. Add ears.

4 Add two more legs. Draw two horns.

5 Add a tail. Draw the inner ear lines. Draw a nose and mouth.

6 Add lines to horns. Make your goat shaggy. Draw hooves. Erase extra lines. Add shading.

Goats are cousins of sheep, but unlike sheep. do not have woolly coats. They are hardier than sheep and can adapt to many different types of environments.

Cow

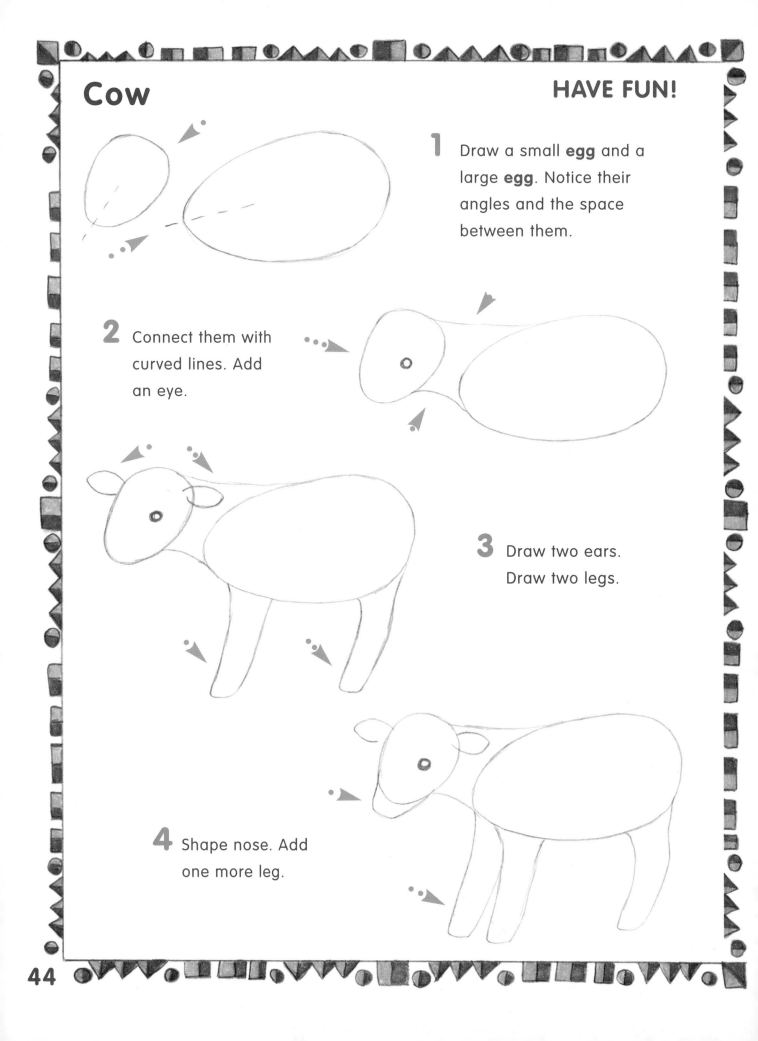

1 Draw a small **egg** and a large **egg**. Notice their angles and the space between them.

2 Connect them with curved lines. Add an eye.

3 Draw two ears. Draw two legs.

4 Shape nose. Add one more leg.

5 Draw a tail. Add the udder.

6 Draw two horns. Add one more leg. Add hooves and the tip of the tail.

7 Add spots. Finish tail. Shade and color.

Cows are famous for giving milk. One cow can give as much as eighty glasses a day. Black and white spotted cows are called Holsteins.

Duck

Webbed feet and oily feathers help a duck be at home in the water.

1 Start with a **circle** and an **egg**.

2 Make curved neck lines. Add an eye.

3 Add a bill. Draw tail feathers. Draw a leg.

4 Draw the wing. Add a webbed foot.

5 Add a second leg and foot. Erase extra lines. Add shading. Draw a pond for your duck to swim in.

Goose

1 Draw a **circle** and an **egg**. Notice the distance between them.

2 Connect head and body with curving neck lines. Add an eye. Draw tail feathers.

3 Add the beak. Make a wing line. Draw two legs.

4 Draw webbed feet. Erase extra lines. Add shading.

A goose is taller than a duck and hardier than a chicken.

Rooster

1 Start with a big **egg** and a small **circle**.

2 Add an eye. Add curved neck lines.

3 Draw the rooster's comb and beak.

4 Add showy tail feathers. Draw wing line. Draw two legs.

5 Draw the rooster's wattle. Add feet.

6 Add neck feathers. Erase extra lines. Add shading and color.

1

2

Chick
Draw a baby chick.

3

Hen

1 Start with a big **egg** and a small **circle**. Notice the angles.

2 Add an eye. Add curved neck lines.

3 Draw a beak. Add a wing line. Draw tail feathers. They are smaller than the rooster's.

4 Make a small comb. Add two legs.

5 Add feet: three toes in front, one in back. Erase extra lines. Add shading and color.

Turkey

1 Start with a very small **circle** and a very big **egg**.

A baby turkey is called a poult. Turkeys have bumpy heads.

2 Add a beak. Draw the eye. Add one neck line. draw two legs.

3 Add feet: three toes in front and one in back.

4 Add the wattle. Add wing feathers.

5 Draw tail feathers. Erase extra lines. Add shading and color.

Horse

1 Start with an **egg** and an **oval**. Notice the angles.

2 Add an eye. Add curved neck lines.

3 Draw the nose and add a nostril.

4 Add a front leg and a hind leg.

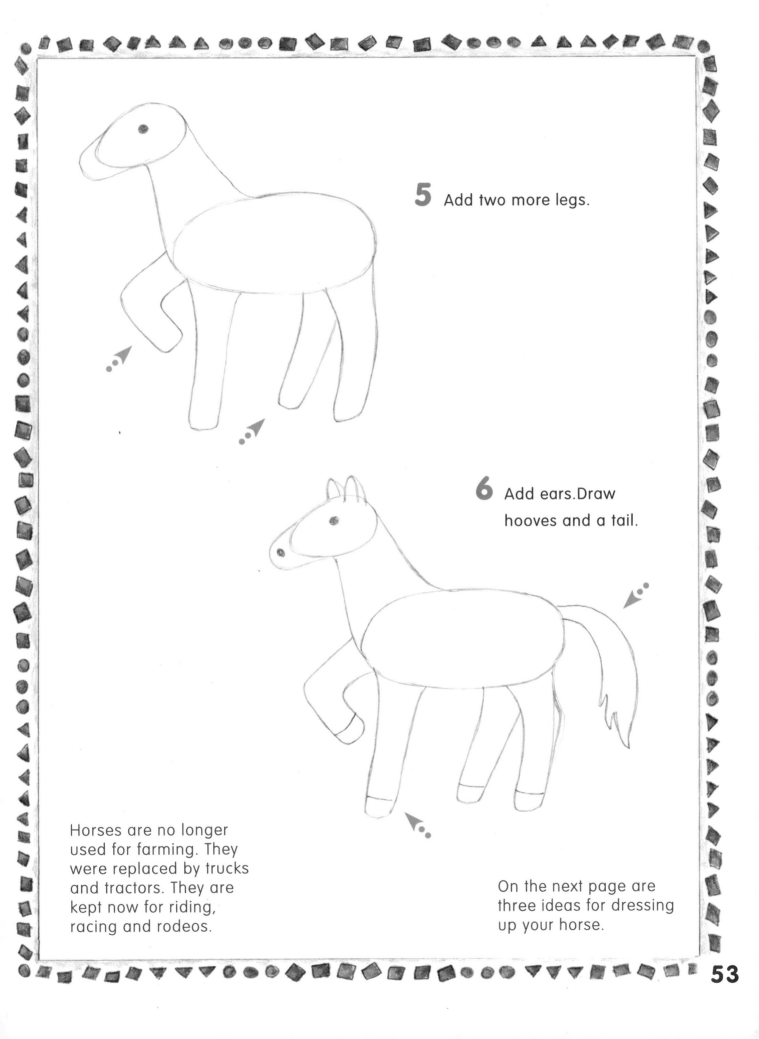

5 Add two more legs.

6 Add ears. Draw hooves and a tail.

Horses are no longer used for farming. They were replaced by trucks and tractors. They are kept now for riding, racing and rodeos.

On the next page are three ideas for dressing up your horse.

Put a saddle and bridle on your dapple gray.

Add a horn to make a unicorn.

Add wings to make a flying horse called Pegasus.

54

Donkey

1 Start with an **oval** and an **egg**. Notice the angles.

2 Add long ears. Add an eye. Draw neck lines.

3 Draw the start of a tail. Draw two legs.

Donkeys are horses' little cousins. They are sure- footed and still used in many places to carry burdens on rocky paths.

Donkey, continued

4 Add a tail tuft. Add a nostril. Draw two more legs.

5 Draw a mane. Draw the inner ear lines. Lengthen the nose. Add hooves.

6 Erase extra lines. Add shading and color.

Bee

1 Draw two **ovals**. Make them **overlap**. Notice the angles.

What a useful friend the bee is! A bee gives us honey and beeswax. It pollinates flowers and helps them grow. Farmers raise bees in apiaries.

2 Draw two eyes.

3 Draw two wings.

4 Draw three legs.

5 Draw a proboscis. Add another leg.

6 Erase extra lines. Add stripes and shading.

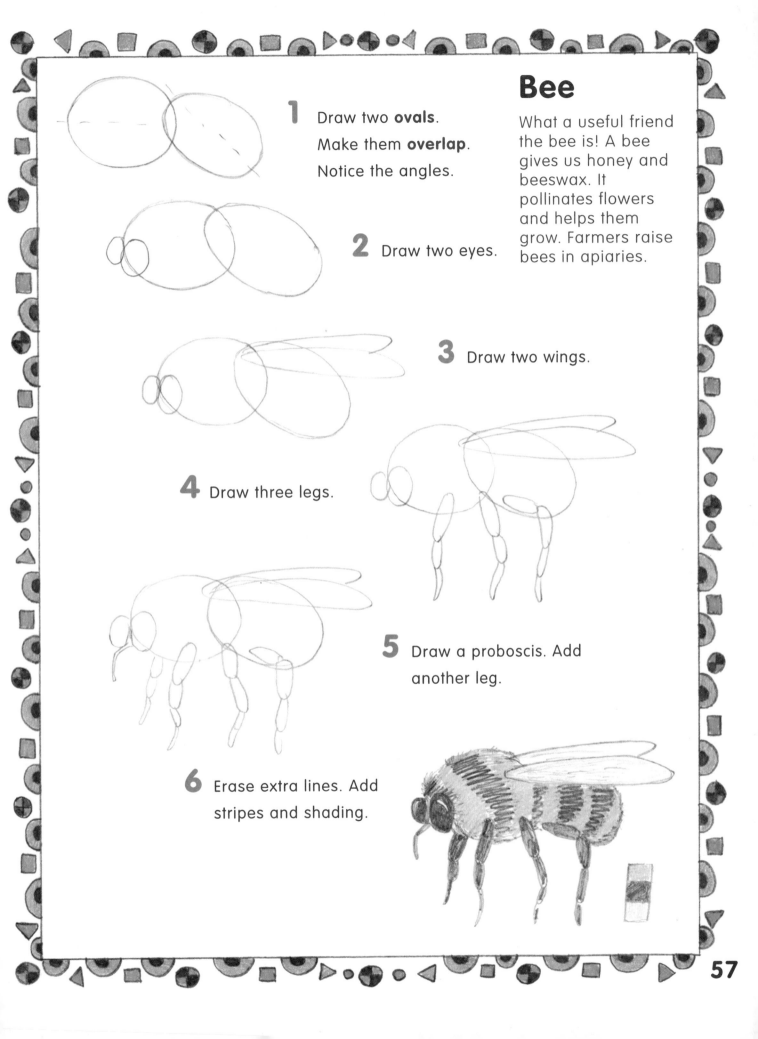

Squirrel

1 Start with three **ovals**: medium, small and large. Notice the angles.

2 Draw two ears. Draw the eye. Draw a curved line connecting neck and back.

3 Add the nose. Draw two curved lines to shape the tummy and the other back leg.

4 Add a line to the nose. Make two front paws and a chest line. Draw a hind foot.

HAVE FUN!

5 Draw a big bushy tail. Add another hind foot.

6 Erase extra lines and shade markings. Make the tail furry.

Super squirrel!

1
2
3

Draw some acorns for your squirrel to bury.

Squirrels are in the rodent family. They are at home in the city or in the country. Always busy, they bury nuts and seeds for winter meals. They don't remember all of them and the forgotten food grows into new plants.

Crow

1 Start with a **circle** and an **egg**. Notice the angles.

2 Add an eye. Draw the neck.

3 Add a beak. Draw a wing.

4 Draw a tail and the tops of legs.

5 Add feather lines. Draw feet. Erase extra lines. Add shading and color.

A large, handsome bird, the crow is all black from head to toe.

Scarecrow

1 Start with a **square** and a **circle**. Make them **overlap**.

2 Add a face. Draw two **rectangles** for the arms.

3 Add two **rectangles** for trousers..

4 Add an **oval** for a hat brim. Draw two legs.

Farmers use scarecrows to keep birds from eating crops.

61

5 Draw the top of the hat. Add two buttons. Draw straw coming out of the sleeves.

6 Put patches on the trousers and a ragged edge. Erase lines. Add shading and color. Add a crow!